Switch Your Light On:

A Guided Journal for Everyday Positivity

Copyright Notice

Switch Your Light On: A Guided Journal for Everyday Positivity
Copyright © 2024 by Nuria Corbi
All rights reserved.

ISBN: 978-1-7394865-5-6

Homeboss Media

For permissions, enquiries, or further information, visit
https://nuriacorbi.com

Introduction

Welcome to Switch Your Light On: A Guided Journal for Everyday Positivity! If you've read my book *The Positivity Switch*, you already know how much I believe in the power of small, intentional changes to transform your mindset and brighten your days. If you haven't read it, no worries— you're in the right place to start creating your own moments of joy, clarity, and resilience.

This journal is your companion on the journey to switching on those mental switches and finding the light even in life's dimmer moments. Think of it as your personal space to reflect, explore, and celebrate all the good stuff—big or small—that makes life meaningful.

Here's the best part: there are no rules here. This journal is yours to use however feels right. Some days you might fill a page with thoughts, doodles, or even an inspired shopping list (hey, positivity can strike anywhere!). Other days, you might just jot down a single word that speaks to you. It's all okay. Progress, not perfection, is the goal.

Each page is designed to nudge you gently toward positivity. You'll find prompts, reflections, and quotes that encourage you to pause, appreciate, and explore what matters most. There's space to dream big, vent a little, and capture those fleeting moments of gratitude, kindness, or just plain old fun.

I hope this journal becomes a little pocket of light in your daily life, a place where you can reconnect with yourself and the things that bring you joy. You don't need to fill it out perfectly or follow it like a rigid schedule—just let it meet you where you are and guide you toward where you want to be.

So grab your favourite pen (or pencil, or crayon—whatever floats your creative boat) and let's get started. Your journey to a brighter mindset begins here. And remember: switching on the light is always within your power.

Here's to the joy of journaling and all the little sparks of positivity it will bring.

With gratitude and a good cup of coffee,

Nuria Corbi

The Seven Switches: A Quick Guide

If you haven't read *The Positivity Switch*, don't worry—this journal works beautifully as a standalone tool. But to give you some context, here's a brief introduction to the seven switches that inspired it. Each switch represents a mindset shift designed to help you bring more positivity into your life:

The Appreciation Switch: Finding joy in the little things and focusing on the good, no matter how small. Gratitude has a way of transforming your perspective.

The Mindfulness Switch: Staying present in the moment instead of worrying about the past or future. Mindfulness keeps you grounded and reduces stress.

The Kindness Switch: Extending kindness to yourself and others, even in tough situations. Small acts of kindness can ripple outward in amazing ways.

The Self-Belief Switch: Building confidence in your abilities, one step at a time. Self-belief is the foundation for pursuing your goals.

The Perspective Switch: Shifting how you see challenges, turning setbacks into opportunities to learn and grow.

The Resilience Switch: Bouncing back stronger from life's challenges. Resilience is the courage to keep going, even when it's tough.

The Visualisation Switch: Picturing your goals clearly and vividly. Visualisation helps you focus on possibilities and take action toward your dreams.

Whether you've read the main book or are discovering these switches for the first time, this journal is here to help you explore and apply these ideas in your daily life. Let's get started!

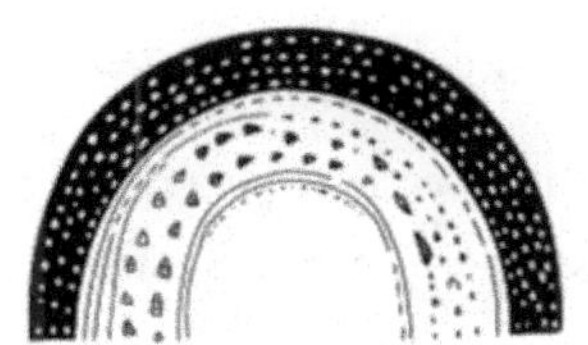

How to Use This Journal

Welcome to Switch Your Light On: A Guided Journal for Everyday Positivity! Whether you're here to spark a little more joy, cultivate clarity, or build resilience, this journal is your personal space to explore, reflect, and grow. There's no right or wrong way to use it—it's all about making it work for you.

Here are a few tips to help you get started:

1. Take It One Page at a Time
Think of this journal as your friendly companion, not a homework assignment. There's no deadline, and you can skip around if something catches your eye. Some days, you might feel like diving deep; other days, a quick jot will do. Both are perfectly fine.

2. Find a Rhythm That Works for You
- Daily Dose of Positivity: Start your morning with gratitude prompts to set the tone for the day, or wind down in the evening with reflections on what went well.
- Weekly Wrap-Ups: At the end of each week, take a moment to pause, reflect, and celebrate your progress.

Even if you miss a day or two (or ten), don't worry—this journal is here when you're ready to jump back in.

3. Make It Yours
Feel free to doodle, sketch, or decorate the pages. This is your journal, and it's meant to reflect your unique journey. Don't be afraid to get creative!

4. Flick the Switches
The prompts in this journal are inspired by the seven switches from The Positivity Switch. Whether it's focusing on gratitude, mindfulness, kindness, or self-belief, each switch is here to guide you toward a brighter, more positive mindset.

5. Celebrate Small Wins
Every entry you write, every insight you gain, is a step forward. Positivity is a practice, not a destination. Give yourself credit for showing up—your light is shining brighter with every page.

6. Keep It Flexible
If a prompt doesn't resonate with you one day, skip it or tweak it to fit your mood. This journal is here to support you, not box you in.

Remember, this isn't about being perfect—it's about showing up for yourself, one little step at a time. Let this journal be a place where you can explore, reflect, and celebrate your journey toward everyday positivity. Now, grab your favourite pen, a cosy spot, and let's get started.

The Appreciation Switch

Noticing Life's Little Gifts

Appreciation is all about shifting your focus to the good that's already present in your life, no matter how small. It's a practice of recognising the moments, people, and experiences that bring you joy and contentment. The Appreciation Switch isn't about pretending everything's perfect - it's about finding light in the ordinary and letting it brighten your day.

Appreciation in Action

This week, we'll explore how to bring more appreciation into your daily life by noticing and valuing the small joys around you.

Day 1: Start Small, See Big

What's one small thing you appreciated today? How did it make you feel?

Exercise: Write a short paragraph about something seemingly insignificant that made you smile - a blooming flower, the sound of laughter, or a moment of quiet.

Quote: "Enjoy the little things, for one day you may look back and realise they were the big things." - Robert Brault

Day 2: Gratitude in Action

Who or what are you most grateful for today, and why?

____

____

____

____

____

____

____

____

____

____

Exercise: Write a thank-you note to someone you appreciate, even if you don't plan to send it. Focus on what they've brought to your life.

Quote: "Appreciation is a wonderful thing. It makes what is excellent in others belong to us as well." - Voltaire

Day 3: Everyday Wonders

What's something ordinary in your daily routine that you often overlook but are actually grateful for?

____

____

____

____

____

____

____

____

____

____

Exercise: Create a list of five "everyday wonders" in your life - things you might take for granted but would miss if they were gone.

Quote: "Appreciation can make a day - even change a life." - Margaret Cousins

Day 4: The Sounds of Appreciation

What's a sound, song, or conversation that brought you joy today? How did it make you feel?

Exercise: Spend 10 minutes listening to something you love - a favourite song, the birds outside, or the hum of a bustling café. Write about the experience.

Quote: "Gratitude paints little smiley faces on everything it touches." — Richelle E. Goodrich

Day 5: Savor the Moment

Think back on a moment today when you felt completely at ease or content. What made it special?

____

____

____

____

____

____

____

____

____

____

Exercise: Take a mindful moment as you sip your next cup of tea or coffee. Savour each sip and write about what you noticed.

Quote: "Happiness is letting go of what you think your life is supposed to look like and celebrating it for everything that it is."
- Mandy Hale

Day 6: Reflecting on the Good

*What are three things you're grateful for from the past week?
How have they shaped your mood or perspective?*

____

____

____

____

____

____

____

____

____

____

*Exercise: Write down these three things and reflect on what
they've taught you about your life and priorities.*

*Quote: "Reflect upon your present blessings - of which every man
has many - not on your past misfortunes, of which all men have
some." - Charles Dickens*

Day 7: Passing It On

How can you share appreciation with someone else today?

Exercise: Perform a small act of kindness as a way to express gratitude - send a message, lend a hand, or simply say "thank you." Reflect on how it felt to give appreciation.

Quote: "Feeling gratitude and not expressing it is like wrapping a present and not giving it." - William Arthur Ward

Final Reflection

Appreciation doesn't require grand gestures or monumental events. It's about recognising the beauty in the everyday and letting it fill your heart. As you practice flicking the Appreciation Switch, you'll discover how much light is already present in your life - and how it grows when you share it with others.

Creative Exercise

Gratitude Jar

Start a "Gratitude Jar." Each day, write down one thing you're grateful for on a small piece of paper and place it in the jar. Over time, you'll have a jar full of positive moments to revisit whenever you need a lift. Use this space to design a label for your jar or list initial ideas to get started.

Appreciation Doodles

Draw or doodle something you're grateful for today. It could be as simple as a steaming cup of tea, a sunny sky, or a hug from a loved one.

The Mindfulness Switch

Being Fully Present

Welcome to The Mindfulness Switch! If life often feels like a whirlwind of to-dos, distractions, and overthinking, this switch is here to help you pause and take a deep breath—literally. Mindfulness is about learning to tune into the moment you're in, letting go of the mental clutter, and grounding yourself in the here and now.

When you're mindful, you notice the small things that often get lost in the shuffle—like the warmth of the sun on your face, the taste of your morning coffee, or even the sound of rain tapping on the window. It's about being where your feet are and finding calm amid the chaos.

Mindfulness in Action

Mindfulness doesn't require you to sit cross-legged on a yoga mat for hours (unless that's your thing). It can be as simple as focusing on your breath for a minute or fully immersing yourself in an activity, like drinking a cup of tea without multitasking.
This week, we'll explore how mindfulness can help you slow down, reduce stress, and reconnect with the present moment.

Day 1: Anchoring Yourself

What's one moment today where you felt fully present? Describe it in detail. What did you notice?

____

____

____

____

____

____

____

____

____

____

Exercise: Pause and take five deep breaths. With each inhale, think, "I am here". With each exhale, think, "I am calm".

Quote: "Mindfulness isn't difficult. We just need to remember to do it." - Sharon Salzberg

Day 2: Noticing the Small Things

Write about three small things you noticed today that made you smile or feel calm.

____

____

____

____

____

____

____

____

____

____

Exercise: Pick a daily activity (e.g., brushing your teeth, eating a meal) and focus fully on it. Pay attention to the sensations, movements, and sounds involved.

Quote: "The present moment is filled with joy and happiness. If you are attentive, you will see it." - Thich Nhat Hanh

Day 3: Embracing Stillness

How does stillness feel to you? Is it peaceful, uncomfortable, or something else? Reflect on what stillness means in your life.

Exercise: Sit quietly for three minutes. Close your eyes, focus on your breath, and let your thoughts come and go without judgment.

Quote: "Be still, and the earth will speak to you." - Navajo Proverb

Day 4: Letting Go of Distractions

*What's one thing that often distracts you? How can you create a
moment of mindfulness despite it?*

____

____

____

____

____

____

____

____

____

____

*Exercise: Put your phone on airplane mode for one hour and
engage in a screen-free activity that brings you joy.*

*Quote: "You can't stop the waves, but you can learn to surf." - Jon
Kabat-Zinn*

Day 5: Finding Peace in the Chaos

Think of a recent chaotic moment. How could mindfulness have helped you navigate it? How can it help you in the future?

Exercise: Practice mindful walking. Go for a short walk and focus on the sensation of your feet on the ground, the rhythm of your steps, and the sounds around you.

Quote: "Mindfulness is the key to a happy, calm mind." - Unknown

Day 6: A Mindful Moment with Someone Else

Describe a time when you were fully present in a conversation.
How did it feel for you and the other person?

____

____

____

____

____

____

____

____

____

____

Exercise: Have a mindful conversation today. Put away
distractions and listen deeply to the person speaking.

Quote: "The most precious gift we can offer others is our presence."
- Thich Nhat Hanh

Day 7: Reflecting on Mindfulness

How has practicing mindfulness this week impacted your mood, energy, or outlook? What surprised you the most?

____

____

____

____

____

____

____

____

____

Exercise: Spend five minutes in mindful gratitude. Close your eyes and think of three things you're grateful for. Focus on how each one makes you feel.

Quote: "Mindfulness is the path to a brighter world within." - Unknown

Final Reflection

Mindfulness is a practice that grows stronger with time. Like a muscle, the more you flex it, the more natural it becomes. Carry the lessons of this week forward, and remember that mindfulness is always just a breath away.

Colour in this mandala to bring yourself into the moment. Focus on the patterns and how the colours make you feel. Use pencils rather than felt tips to avoid bleedthrough to the next page.

The Visualisation Switch

Picturing Possibilities

Have you ever noticed how much easier it is to achieve something when you can clearly see it in your mind first? That's the magic of visualisation.

The Visualisation Switch is all about imagining your goals, dreams, and possibilities with such vivid clarity that they almost feel real. When you picture the life you want, you start aligning your actions to make it happen - like a mental satnav pointing you in the right direction.

Visualisation in Action

This week, we'll focus on creating vivid, powerful mental pictures of your dreams and learning how to use those images as motivation to move forward.

Day 1: Dream Big, Start Small

Imagine your dream life - where you live, what you do, how you feel. What's one small step you could take today to move closer to that vision?

____

____

____

____

____

____

____

____

____

____

____

Exercise: Write a short story about your life five years from now. Include as much detail as possible about what you see, hear, and feel.

Quote: "If you can dream it, you can do it." — Walt Disney

Day 2: Visualise Your Day

Before your day begins, take a moment to imagine how you'd like it to unfold. What would make today feel successful or joyful?

Exercise: Sketch or write a timeline of your ideal day, from morning to evening. Picture yourself accomplishing your tasks with ease and enjoyment.

Quote: "Visualisation is daydreaming with a purpose."

Day 3: Turning Dreams into Goals

Choose one dream you've had for a long time. What specific steps would you need to take to make it a reality?

____

____

____

____

____

____

____

____

____

____

Exercise: Break your dream into three actionable goals. Write these down and visualise yourself achieving each one.

Quote: "A goal without a plan is just a wish." - Antoine de Saint-Exupéry

Day 4: Vision Boards with a Twist

What images, words, or symbols inspire you? How do they reflect the life you want to create?

____

____

____

____

____

____

____

____

____

____

____

Exercise: Create a mini vision board. Use magazine clippings, drawings, or even a Pinterest board to bring your goals to life visually.

Quote: "The clearer your vision, the stronger your focus."

Day 5: See It, Feel It, Believe It

Visualisation works best when it feels real. What emotions would you experience if your dream life became reality?

____

____

____

____

____

____

____

____

____

____

Exercise: Spend five minutes imagining yourself achieving a specific goal. Focus on the emotions, sounds, and sensations you'd experience.

Quote: "See it in your mind and hold it in your hand."

Day 6: Overcoming Obstacles

Visualisation isn't just about picturing success - it's also about imagining how you'll overcome challenges. What's one obstacle standing between you and your goal? How can you navigate it?

Exercise: Write a step-by-step plan for tackling one specific challenge. Visualise yourself overcoming it with confidence.

Quote: "Obstacles are what you see when you take your eyes off the goal."

Day 7: Reflecting on Visualisation

After a week of visualisation, what have you noticed? Do you feel more motivated, focused, or hopeful?

____

____

____

____

____

____

____

____

____

____

Exercise: Write a thank-you note to yourself for taking the time to dream and plan. Include one visualisation you're excited to keep working on.

Quote: "Your imagination is your preview of life's coming attractions." — Albert Einstein

Final Reflection

Visualisation is more than daydreaming - it's about creating a mental blueprint for the life you want to build. By focusing on your goals and picturing yourself achieving them, you're setting the stage for real-world success. Remember, the clearer your vision, the more power it has to inspire your actions.

Dreamscape Doodles

Draw your dream life. Include anything that makes you happy - your ideal home, career, hobbies or moments of joy.

Your imagination is your canvas.

Vision Board

Doodle or paste clippings of things you want to manifest.

Draw your vision: from dreams to reality!

The Kindness Switch

Spreading Goodness, One Gesture at a Time

Kindness isn't just something you do for others—it's a gift that comes right back to you. The Kindness Switch is all about those small, thoughtful gestures that can turn someone's day around (including your own). From a warm smile to lending a helping hand, kindness creates ripples of positivity that extend far beyond the initial act.

When you flick this switch, you'll find that kindness has a way of lifting your spirits too. It's like the ultimate two-for-one deal: you brighten someone else's world and feel pretty fantastic about it yourself.

Kindness in Action

Kindness doesn't need to be grand or costly. Sometimes, it's as simple as holding a door open, sending a kind message, or listening with your full attention. This week, let's dive into how small acts of kindness can create big waves of positivity.

Day 1: Starting Small

Think about a time when someone's kindness brightened your day. How did it make you feel?

____

____

____

____

____

____

____

____

____

____

Exercise: Perform one small act of kindness today - hold a door open, share a compliment, or offer to help someone in need.

Quote: "No act of kindness, no matter how small, is ever wasted."
- Aesop

Day 2: Kindness Towards Yourself

What's one way you can show kindness to yourself today? Write about why you deserve it.

____

____

____

____

____

____

____

____

____

____

Exercise: Treat yourself to something small that make you happy - a quiet moment, a favourite snack, or even saying no to something you don't want to do.

Quote: "Be kind to yourself. You're doing the best you can." - Unknown

Day 3: Noticing Opportunities

Where in your daily life do you see opportunities for small acts of kindness? How can you take advantage of them?

____

____

____

____

____

____

____

____

____

____

Exercise: Make a conscious effort to look for ways to be kind throughout the day. Note one opportunity you acted on.

Quote: "Kindness is seeing the best in others when they cannot see it in themselves." - Unknown

Day 4: Spreading Joy

Write about a time when your kindness had a noticeable impact on someone else. How did it make you feel?

____

____

____

____

____

____

____

____

____

____

____

Exercise: Send an encouraging message to someone - a friend, family member, or even an acquaintance. Let them know you're thinking of them.

Quote: "Sometimes it takes only one act of kindness to change a person's life." - Unknown

Day 5: Unexpected Kindness

*Describe a time when you received kindness from a stranger.
What did it teach you about the power of kindness?*

---

*Exercise: Do something for someone you don't know - a stranger at
the shop, someone in traffic, or even a neighbour you've never
spoken to.*

*Quote: "The world is full of kind people. If you can't find one, be
one." - Unknown*

Day 6: Kindness in Tough Moments

Think about a time when it was hard to be kind, but you chose to be anyway. What was the outcome?

____

____

____

____

____

____

____

____

____

____

____

Exercise: The next time you encounter a frustrating situation, take a deep breath and respond with kindness instead of frustration.

Quote: "A gentle word, a kind look, a good-natured smle can work wonders and accomplish miracles." William Hazlitt

Day 7: Reflecting on Kindness

How has practising kindness this week impacted your relationships, mood, or perspective?

____

____

____

____

____

____

____

____

____

____

Exercise: Take a moment to reflect on how kindness has spread through your actions this week. Write down one thing you've learned about yourself in the process.

____

____

____

Quote: "Kindness begins with the understanding that we all struggle." - Charles Glassman

Final Reflection

The Kindness Switch reminds us that small, thoughtful actions can make a big difference - not just for others, but for ourselves too. Whether you're showing kindness to a stranger, a loved one, or yourself, every act creates ripples of positivity that brighten the world.

Acts of Kindness Tree

Draw a tree and label each branch with an act of kindness you've done or plan to do. Add leaves or fruit for each act completed.

Kindness Jar

Fill a jar with little pieces of paper where you write an act of kindness that you have performed. It can be something really small, it all counts. You can also write them into this jar.

The Self-Belief Switch

Unlocking Your Inner Confidence

Let's be honest - believing in yourself can feel like a bit of a stretch on some days. You know, those mornings when even your coffee seems unimpressed with your life choices? But here's the thing: self-belief isn't something you're born with. It's a skill, one that grows stronger every time you take a step forward, even if it's a tiny, wobbly one.

The Self-Belief Switch is about quieting that inner critic and turning up the volume on the voice that says, *"You've got this."* Because, let's face it, you absolutely do.

Self-Belief in Action

Self-belief doesn't mean you'll never have doubts - it means you'll keep going anyway. This week, we'll work on building confidence, one small, empowering step at a time.

Day 1: Starting Small

Write about a time when you surprised yourself by accomplishing something you didn't think you could. How did it feel?

____

____

____

____

____

____

____

____

____

____

Exercise: Pick one small thing you've been putting off and do it today. Remind yourself that every little win counts.

Quote: "Whether you think you can or you think you can't, you're right." - Henry Ford

Day 2: The Power of Affirmation

What's one thing you like about yourself? Write about why it makes you proud.

Exercise: Stand in front of a mirror (yes, really!) and say out loud one positive thing about yourself. Repeat it three times. No eye-rolling allowed.

Quote: "You are braver than you believe, stronger than you seem, and smarter than you think." - A.A. Milne

Day 3: Celebrating Progress

Think about a goal you've been working towards. What progress have you made, even if it's small?

____

____

____

____

____

____

____

____

____

____

____

Exercise: Write down three steps you've taken towards your goal, no matter how minor they seem. Celebrate each one - you've earned it!

____

____

____

____

Quote: "Success is the sum of small efforts repeated day in and day out." - Robert Collier

Day 4: Quieting the Inner Critic

What's one negative thought you often tell yourself? How could you reframe it into something more supportive?

Exercise: Every time your inner critic speaks up today, counter it with a positive affirmation. (For example, "I'm not good at this" becomes "I'm learning and improving every day.")

Quote: "Talk to yourself like you would to someone you love." - Brené Brown

Day 5: Learning from Setbacks

Write about a setback that initially felt like a failure but ultimately taught you something valuable.

Exercise: Identify one lesson you've learned from a recent challenge. Reflect on how it has made you stronger or wiser.

Quote: "Failure is simply the opportunity to begin again, this time more intelligently." - Henry Ford

Day 6: Surrounding Yourself with Positivity

Who in your life inspires you to believe in yourself? Write about how they've impacted you.

Exercise: Reach out to someone who's been a positive influence in your life. Thank them and let them know how much they mean to you.

Quote: "Surround yourself with people who believe in your dreams." - Unknown

Day 7: Reflecting on Growth

How has focusing on self-belief this week changed your perspective on what you're capable of?

____

____

____

____

____

____

____

____

____

____

____

Exercise: Write a letter to your future self, celebrating the confidence you've built and encouraging yourself to keep growing.

Quote: "Believe you can, and you're halfway there." - Theodore Roosevelt

Final Reflection

The Self-Belief Switch reminds us that confidence isn't about never doubting yourself - it's about choosing to trust in your abilities, even when doubt tries to sneak in. With every small step, you're building a foundation of strength, courage, and unstoppable determination.

Confidence Badge

Design a badge or emblem that represents your unique strengths and achievements. What symbols or colours reflect your self-belief?

The Perspective Switch

Seeing the Bigger Picture

Ah, perspective - it's the magical ability to take a step back, squint at the situation, and realise that maybe, just maybe, it's not the end of the world. The Perspective Switch is like having a built-in compass that helps you navigate life's ups and downs by showing you new angles and hidden opportunities.

Sometimes, we get so caught up in the moment that a challenge feels bigger than it really is. But with a little shift in perspective, what once felt like a mountain can suddenly seem more like a molehill - or at least a moderately-sized hill.

Perspective in Action

This week, we'll explore how to reframe challenges, find silver linings, and embrace the lessons that come with life's twists and turns.

Day 1: Reframing Challenges

Think of a recent challenge you faced. How might someone else see it differently? What's one good thing that could come out of it?

Exercise: Write down three possible lessons or opportunities that could arise from this challenge.

Quote: "We can complain because rose bushes have thorns, or rejoice because thorns have roses." - Alphonse Karr

Day 2: A New Lens

Recall a time when a setback turned out to be a blessing in disguise. How did it change your perspective?

____

____

____

____

____

____

____

____

____

____

Exercise: Practice seeing the good in a frustrating situation today. What's one positive takeaway you can find?

Quote: "Sometimes the best thing you can do is look at it from another angle."

Day 3: Zooming Out

Imagine your current worries from the perspective of your future self. Will they matter in five or ten years? Why or why not?

Exercise: Write a letter from your future self, offering advice and reassurance about your current challenges.

Quote: "What seems important now may one day be just a footnote in your story."

Day 4: The Power of Gratitude

How does practising gratitude change your perspective on difficult situations? Write about a challenge you're grateful for and why.

Exercise: Choose one thing you're struggling with and write three reasons you're thankful for the experience (even if it's a stretch!).

Quote: "Gratitude turns what we have into enough."

Day 5: Stepping into Someone Else's Shoes

Think of a time when someone else's perspective helped you see things differently. How did it change your approach?

____

____

____

____

____

____

____

____

____

____

Exercise: Have a conversation with someone who has a different viewpoint on a topic that's been on your mind. Listen with curiosity, not judgment.

Quote: "Sometimes all you need is a fresh pair of eyes."

Day 6: Celebrating Small Wins

How can shifting your focus to what's going well change your perspective? Write about three small wins you've had recently.

____

____

____

____

____

____

____

____

____

____

Exercise: Take a moment to celebrate one of these small victories today - treat yourself to something that makes you smile.

Quote: "Perspective turns small wins into stepping stones."

Day 7: Reflecting on Growth

How has focusing on perspective this week helped you reframe challenges or find new opportunities?

____

____

____

____

____

____

____

____

____

____

Exercise: Write a short note to yourself about how changing your perspective has impacted your mindset and actions.

Quote: "Change the way you look at things, and the things you look at change." - Wayne Dyer

Final Reflection

The Perspective Switch teaches us that life isn't just about what
happens - it's about how we choose to see it. By shifting our
viewpoint, we open ourselves to new possibilities, fresh ideas, and
unexpected silver linings.

Reframe Map

Draw a situation you're facing from a bird's-eye view. Add symbols or notes showing how you can reframe it to see the opportunity instead of the obstacle. Give it a go!

The Resilience Switch

Rising Stronger

Resilience - it's that quiet, determined part of you that says, "*I've got this,*" even when life feels like it's testing you at every turn. The Resilience Switch is all about bouncing back, learning from challenges, and finding the strength to keep going. Think of it as your inner superhero cape - sometimes it's tucked away, but it's always there when you need it.

Resilience in Action

This week, we'll focus on recognising your inner strength, reflecting on past victories, and building the kind of resilience that turns setbacks into comebacks.

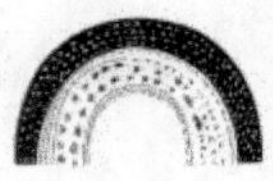

Day 1: Strength Trough Challenges

Think of a difficult time in your life that you overcame. What helped you get through it, and what did you learn from the experience?

____

____

____

____

____

____

____

____

____

____

Exercise: Write a letter to your past self, thanking them for their strength and determination during that tough time.

Quote: "You never know how strong you are until being strong is your only choice." - Bob Marley

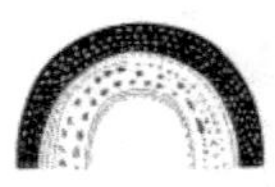

Day 2: Bouncing Back

What's one recent setback you've faced? How did you handle it, and what could you do differently next time?

____

____

____

____

____

____

____

____

____

____

Exercise: Write down three ways you've grown or changed as a result of past challenges.

Quote: "Fall seven times, stand up eight." — Japanese Proverb

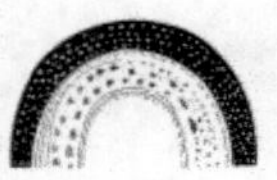

Day 3: The Silver Lining

Reflect on a moment when something that seemed negative at first turned out to be a blessing in disguise. How did it shape who you are today?

Exercise: Choose a current challenge and list three potential silver linings or opportunities it could lead to.

Quote: "The storm makes you appreciate the sunshine."

Day 4: Building Your Resilience Toolkit

What tools, habits, or practices help you stay grounded during tough times? How can you lean on these more often?

____

____

____

____

____

____

____

____

____

____

Exercise: Create a "resilience toolkit" by listing five things you can do when life feels overwhelming (e.g., deep breathing, talking to a friend, taking a walk).

Quote: "Resilience is knowing that you are the only one who has the power and the responsibility to pick yourself up." - Mary Holloway

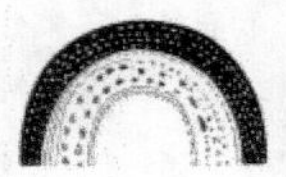

Day 5: Celebrating Small Victories

Resilience often grows from small wins. What's one small victory you can celebrate today? How does it remind you of your ability to persevere?

____

____

____

____

____

____

____

____

____

Exercise: Treat yourself to something that feels good - a quiet moment, a cup of tea, or a favourite song - and acknowledge it as a reward for your resilience.

Quote: "Small steps lead to big changes."

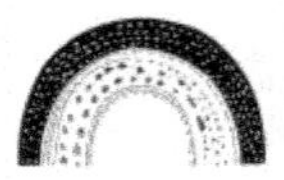

Day 6: Learning to Bend, Not Break

How do you handle stress? What's one way you can adapt or shift your mindset to better manage life's pressures?

Exercise: Write down one area of your life where you can "bend" (adapt or compromise) instead of feeling stuck or rigid.

Quote: "The oak fought the wind and was broken, the willow bent when it must and survived." — Robert Jordan

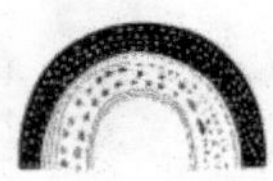

Day 7: Reflecting on Resilience

What does resilience mean to you now, after a week of exploring it? How have you seen your inner strength grow over time?

Exercise: Write a note to your future self, reminding them of the strength you've discovered and how you can always rely on it.

Quote: "You may not control all the events that happen to you, but you can decide not to be reduced by them." - Maya Angelou

Final Reflection

Resilience is the art of rising stronger after every fall. It's not about never feeling down - it's about knowing you can and will get back up.

By focusing on your inner strength and learning to adapt, you're building a foundation that will carry you through life's storms and into brighter days.

Welcome to Your Positivity Roadmap

Congratulations on completing your journey through the seven switches! By now, you've explored appreciation, mindfulness, visualisation, kindness, self-belief, perspective, and resilience - and hopefully, you've felt a spark of transformation along the way.

But positivity isn't just about one-time actions; it's a lifelong journey. That's where the Positivity Roadmap comes in. This section is designed to help you take everything you've learned and dive even deeper. Think of it as your personal guide to creating lasting change, one meaningful step at a time.

The Positivity Roadmap offers a series of guided reflections, activities, and prompts to help you integrate the switches into every area of your life.

Whether you're navigating challenges, planning for the future, or simply looking to grow, this roadmap is here to support you.

Take your time with these pages. There's no rush to finish them all in one sitting. Use them whenever you need clarity, motivation, or a gentle nudge to keep going. This is your journey, and the roadmap is here to help you chart your own unique path toward a brighter, more positive life.

Remember, positivity isn't about being perfect—it's about making intentional choices to focus on the light, even when the road feels dim. You've already come so far, and I can't wait for you to see where the next steps will take you.

Let's switch on the light and keep moving forward!

Section 1: Setting Your Compass

Reflection: Where Are You Now?
Before you plan where you're going, it's important to take stock of where you are. This reflection will help you identify your current mindset, strengths, and areas where you'd like to grow.

Prompt:
Take a moment to reflect on your current state of mind. How do you feel about your life overall? Are there areas where you feel stuck or could use a boost of positivity?

____

____

____

____

____

____

____

____

____

____

____

____

____

____

Section 1: Setting Your Compass

Draw a simple compass on a sheet of paper or use the one below. Label the four points with these categories: Mindset, Relationships, Goals, and Self-Care.

- Under Mindset, write down one word that describes your current outlook (e.g., optimistic, overwhelmed, curious).
- For Relationships, note one area where you feel connected or disconnected.
- Under Goals, write a short sentence about something you're working toward.
- For Self-Care, jot down one thing you're currently doing—or not doing—that impacts your well-being.

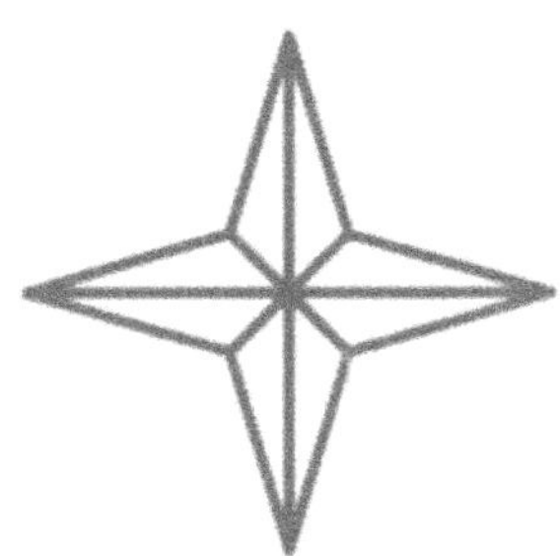

"Knowing yourself is the beginning of all wisdom." — Aristotle

Section 1: Setting Your Compass

Task: Choosing Your Destination

Now that you know where you stand, let's decide where you'd like to go. Think of this as setting your destination on your positivity journey.

Prompt:
What does a positive life look like to you? Describe your "destination" in a few sentences.

____

____

____

____

____

Exercise:
Write a short letter to your future self, describing the life you want to create. Be as specific as possible. Include details about how you'd like to feel, the relationships you'd like to nurture, and the goals you'd like to achieve.

____

____

____

____

____

____

____

____

Takeaway Reflection:
By understanding where you are and where you want to go, you've taken the first step toward a more intentional, positive life.

Section 2: Clearing the Path

Reflection: What's Holding You Back?
Every journey has obstacles, and the key to progress is recognising them. This reflection will help you identify what might be slowing you down or standing in your way.

Prompt:
What's currently holding you back from embracing positivity? Is it self-doubt, fear, a busy schedule, or perhaps external negativity?

____

____

____

____

____

____

____

____

____

____

____

____

____

____

____

Section 2: Clearing the Path

Draw a simple road on the page and label it with your obstacles - think of potholes or roadblocks that you might encounter. For each obstacle, jot down one way you could navigate or overcome it.
For example:
- Obstacle: Lack of time
- Solution: Set aside 10 minutes each morning for reflection.

"Obstacles don't block the path; they are the path." — Zen Proverb

Section 3: Mapping the Journey

Define Your Vision: Where Do You Want to Go?

Every journey starts with a dream—a vision of where you want to go and what you want to achieve. But here's the thing: your vision doesn't have to be grand or world-changing (unless you want it to be!). It just has to be yours. This is your chance to imagine your ideal destination, whether it's a more peaceful mindset, stronger relationships, or a big life goal.

Close your eyes for a moment and ask yourself:

- What does my happiest, most positive self look like?
- How do I want to feel each day?
- What would a truly fulfilling life mean to me?

Once you've got a rough idea, we're going to start turning it into something vivid and motivating. Let's begin.

Section 3: Mapping the Journey

Imagine you've woken up six months from now, and everything feels right in your world. What's different? Write a description of what you see, hear, feel, and experience in this ideal version of your life.

____

____

____

____

____

____

Exercise:
Sketch or write a "mind map" of your vision. Draw or list the key elements that make up your ideal life—think about your environment, relationships, mindset, or achievements.

Takeaway Reflection:
Your vision is your personal compass, guiding you toward the life you want to create. It doesn't have to be perfect or fully formed—it just has to inspire you. Take a moment to trust your instincts and dream boldly, knowing that every journey begins with imagining what's possible.

Section 3: Mapping the Journey

Set Your Destination

Now that you've envisioned the life you want, it's time to zoom in and set clear, tangible goals. Think of this as marking your destination on the map—it gives you something specific to aim for. Big dreams are built on smaller milestones, and each step you define will bring your vision closer to reality.

Defining Your Destination

What does success look like to you? Imagine you've achieved your vision—how will you know you've arrived? Be as specific as possible. For example, instead of "I want to be happier," you might write, "I'll feel happier when I spend more quality time with my family, laugh more, and prioritise self-care."

____

____

____

____

____

____

____

____

____

____

____

____

____

____

Section 3: Mapping the Journey

Exercise: Goal Setting Made Simple

Break your vision into three key areas of focus. For example:

- Personal Growth: What skills or habits will you develop?
- Relationships: How will you nurture connections with loved ones?
- Career or Creativity: What achievements or projects will you pursue?

Write one specific goal for each area.

Section 4: Navigating Challenges

Every great journey comes with its fair share of detours and roadblocks. But here's the thing—challenges don't have to stop you in your tracks. They're opportunities to learn, adapt, and grow stronger. In this section, we'll focus on how to face obstacles head-on with resilience, creativity, and a healthy dose of self-belief.

Think about your goals and the path ahead. What challenges or obstacles might you encounter? Are there specific fears, habits, or external circumstances that could slow you down? Write down a few potential roadblocks, and be honest with yourself.

Section 4: Navigating Challenges

Exercise: Build Your Resilience Toolkit

For each challenge you've identified, brainstorm one or two strategies to overcome it. Here are a few examples:
- Challenge: Lack of time.
  Strategy: Schedule 30 minutes daily for your goal and treat it as non-negotiable.
- Challenge: Self-doubt.
  Strategy: Create a list of your past achievements to remind yourself of your capabilities.
- Challenge: Fear of failure.
  Strategy: Reframe failure as feedback—what can you learn from the experience?

Write your strategies down and refer to them whenever you need a boost.

____

____

____

____

____

____

____

____

____

____

____

Section 4: Navigating Challenges

Reflection: Embrace the Journey

What's one challenge you've overcome in the past that makes you feel proud?
Reflect on how you navigated that situation and the strengths you discovered
in yourself. How can you apply those same strengths to your current goals?

____

____

____

____

____

____

____

____

____

____

____

____

____

____

____

Takeaway Reflection: Navigating Challenges
"Challenges don't block the road; they are the road. Each one you face and
overcome is a step closer to your destination. With the right mindset and
strategies, every roadblock becomes a building block for success."

Section 5: Celebrating the Milestones

The journey to positivity and growth isn't just about the destination—it's about recognising and celebrating every step forward, no matter how small. Each milestone you reach is proof of your progress, a reminder of your resilience, and an opportunity to reflect on how far you've come.

Recognising Your Wins
Take a moment to think about a recent accomplishment, big or small. It could be finishing a tough project, finding a moment of calm in a hectic day, or simply showing up for yourself. What did this win mean to you, and how did it make you feel? Write down your thoughts.

____

____

____

____

____

____

____

____

____

____

____

"Celebrate what you've accomplished, but raise the bar a little higher each time you succeed." — Mia Hamm

Section 5: Celebrating the Milestones

Exercise: Your Celebration Plan
1. Create a Milestone List
2. Look back on your journey so far and identify three milestones you're proud of. Write them down.
3. Plan a Celebration for Each
4. For each milestone, decide how you'll celebrate. It doesn't have to be elaborate—a small treat, a quiet moment of gratitude, or sharing your success with someone you trust can be just as meaningful.

____

____

____

____

____

Reflection: Pause, Reflect, Rejoice
Think about how celebrating your milestones can keep you motivated. How does recognising your wins impact your mindset and your approach to future challenges? Write down how you'll continue to acknowledge your progress moving forward.

____

____

____

____

____

Section 6: Reflecting on the Journey

As you near the end of this guided roadmap, it's time to pause and reflect on everything you've learned, felt, and accomplished. Reflection isn't just about looking back—it's about gaining insight, recognising growth, and setting intentions for the path ahead. Every step you've taken has contributed to your personal story of positivity and resilience.

Looking Back with Gratitude
Think about where you started and where you are now. What shifts have you noticed in your mindset, actions, or outlook? What are you most grateful for from this journey? Write down your reflections.

____

____

____

____

____

____

____

____

____

____

____

____

____

"It's not the destination, but the journey that shapes us." — Unknown

Section 6: Reflecting on the Journey

Exercise: Your Journey Snapshot

1. The High Points

   List three moments or experiences from this roadmap that felt partcularly meaningful or impactful. What made these moments stand out?

2. The Lessons Learned

   Write down one key takeaway from each of the seven switches. How have these lessons shaped the way you approach your life?

3. The Gratitude Note

   Write a short note of gratitude to yourself for committing to this journey. What are you most proud of?

Section 6: Reflecting on the Journey

Reflection: Carrying Positivity Forward
As you reflect on your progress, consider how you'll carry what you've learned into your daily life. What habits or practices will you continue? How will you remind yourself of your growth when challenges arise? Write your thoughts as a commitment to yourself.

____

____

____

____

____

____

____

____

____

____

____

____

____

____

____

____

Interactive Lists

Bucket List: Write 10 things you always wanted to try and why.

Interactive Lists

Kindness List: Brainstorm 20 small acts of kndness you could do.

Interactive Lists

Dream List: List five goals you've been putting off. What's one step you could take today to get closer?

Role Models

Who inspires you to stay positive, and what can you learn from them?

Celebration Page

List five wins - big or small - that deserve celebration.

Check-In Page

How are you feeling today compared to when you started this journal?

Shopping for Positivity

Welcome to the Positivity Market—a magical place where the shelves are stocked with all the good vibes, uplifting energy, and heartwarming moments you could ever need. Your task? Fill your cart with whatever brings you joy, inspiration, and a brighter outlook.

How It Works:
1. Grab Your Basket: Imagine you're walking through this extraordinary shop.
2. Browse the Aisles: Think about the things, feelings, or moments that make your heart lighter and your mind brighter.
3. Fill Your Cart: Write or sketch your "purchases" below. Be as creative as you like!

Positivity isn't something you find—it's something you create. Fill your life with what lifts you up!

Shopping for Positivity

What's in Your Basket?
- A candle of calm for peaceful evenings.
- A box of motivation for tackling those to-do lists.
- A handful of patience for life's little challenges.
- A sunbeam in a bottle for rainy days.
- A book of dreams to inspire your next steps.
- A bundle of courage for trying something new.

Use the space below to add your own items! What do you need to "shop" for today?

Remember: The best things in life can't always be bought—but they can always be imagined!

The Kindness Kiosk

Step up to the Kindness Kiosk, where the currency is compassion, and every purchase spreads joy. Whether you're buying for yourself or someone else, there's always something worth giving.

Here are some coupons to use in your kiosk.

Remember: The best things in life can't always be bought—but they can always be imagined!

Positivity Toolbox

Life can throw all sorts of challenges our way, but with the right tools, we can tackle them head-on. Your Positivity Toolbox is a collection of practical, uplifting strategies designed to help you navigate tough moments and make the most of the good ones.

Whether you're tightening up your self-belief or patching up a difficult day with resilience, these tools are here to remind you that positivity is always within reach. So, grab a "hammer" of gratitude or a "wrench" of kindness, and let's build a brighter outlook together!

"The Gratitude Hammer"
Use this tool to break through negative thoughts by naming three things you're grateful for.
"Feeling stuck in a bad mood? Smash through it with a quick gratitude list. Simple, effective, and it never goes dull!"

"The Kindness Wrench"
Tighten the bolts of connection with an act of kindness.
"Feeling disconnected? A small gesture like writing a thank-you note or offering a helping hand can bring everything back into alignment."

"The Self-Belief Screwdriver"
Turn doubt into determination, one thought at a time.
"Use this tool to remind yourself of a recent win or a challenge you overcame. Tighten up your confidence—it's stronger than you think!"

Remember: The best things in life can't always be bought—but they can always be imagined!

A Helping Hand for Your Positivity Journey

Sometimes, when faced with a blank page or a tricky question, our minds do a disappearing act, leaving us staring at nothing but white space. It's completely normal—life gets busy, and inspiration doesn't always strike when we want it to.

That's why this appendix is here: to give you a little nudge when you need it most. Whether you're finding it hard to think of what you're grateful for, a past challenge you've overcome, or how to shift your perspective, these example lists are designed to spark your thoughts and get the ideas flowing.

Think of them as gentle companions, guiding you through your reflections and helping you make the most of this journal. Remember, there's no right or wrong here—just inspiration to help you along the way. Let's dive in!

A Helping Hand for Your Positivity Journey

Examples for Gratitude Prompts
Feeling stuck on what to be grateful for? Don't worry, we've got you covered. Here's a mix of big blessings and small joys to help you find your gratitude groove.

Big Things to Be Grateful For:
- Supportive family or friends
- A comfortable home
- Good health or access to healthcare
- A job or source of income
- Educational opportunities

Small Everyday Joys:
- A sunny day or beautiful weather
- A good cup of tea or coffee
- A kind smile from a stranger
- Finding a great parking spot
- The sound of birds chirping in the morning

Memorable Moments:
- A recent holiday or trip
- A heartwarming compliment you received
- A family gathering or dinner with friends
- A surprise act of kindness
- A personal or professional achievement

A Helping Hand for Your Positivity Journey

Examples for Resilience Prompts
Sometimes, it's hard to see how far you've come. Use this list to jog your memory and reflect on the challenges you've faced and conquered like the resilient star you are.

Examples for Resilience Prompts
Challenges You've Overcome:
- Completing a difficult project at work
- Recovering from an illness or injury
- Learning a new skill or passing an exam
- Getting through a tough financial period
- Supporting a friend or family member through a hard time

Lessons Learned from Setbacks:
- Realising the value of patience when things didn't go as planned
- Learning to ask for help when overwhelmed
- Gaining confidence after pushing through a fear
- Discovering your strength in a difficult relationship
- Finding new opportunities after a job loss

A Helping Hand for Your Positivity Journey

Examples for Kindness Prompts
Kindness is everywhere—both given and received. If you're struggling to think of examples, these ideas might spark a memory or inspire your next act of kindness.

Examples for Kindness Prompts
Acts of Kindness to Give:
- Compliment someone on their outfit or smile
- Write a thank-you note to a teacher or mentor
- Hold the door open for someone
- Offer to help a neighbour with groceries or chores
- Listen without interrupting when a friend needs to talk

Acts of Kindness You've Received:
- Someone helped you fix something you couldn't do on your own
- A stranger letting you go ahead in a queue
- A handwritten card or thoughtful message
- A friend showing up unexpectedly to cheer you up
- Someone lending you something you needed without hesitation

A Helping Hand for Your Positivity Journey

Examples for Visualisation Prompts
Struggling to picture your dream life? Or maybe the obstacles ahead feel like a blank wall? Use these ideas as a starting point to create your mental masterpiece.

Examples for Visualisation Prompts
Dreams to Visualise:

- Starting your own business or pursuing a creative passion
- Travelling to a dream destination
- Finding the perfect home
- Achieving a major milestone like a degree or certification
- Building stronger relationships with loved ones

Obstacles to Visualise Overcoming:

- Getting through a difficult work presentation
- Facing a fear, like public speaking or flying
- Staying calm during a conflict or argument
- Rebuilding after a financial setback
- Gaining confidence in a new role or challenge

A Helping Hand for Your Positivity Journey

Examples for Perspective Prompts
Finding the silver lining isn't always easy. If you're feeling stuck, these examples can help shift your perspective and reveal the hidden opportunities in life's challenges.

Examples for Perspective Prompts
Shifting Perspective on Challenges:
- Missing out on a job but realising it wasn't the right fit
- A delayed flight that gave you time to read a book
- A failed project that taught you valuable lessons
- A disagreement that deepened your understanding of another's perspective
- A tough year that strengthened your relationships

Silver Linings in Everyday Life:
- Rainy days that make cosy indoor moments more enjoyable
- A mistake at work that sparked creative solutions
- Losing something small and finding something better in its place
- A cancelled plan that gave you time to rest
- An unexpected detour that led to a great discovery

A Final Note: Keep Your Light Shining

As you close this journal, take a moment to pause and celebrate yourself. You've invested time and energy into exploring the switches that brighten your days, and that's no small achievement. Each page you've filled, every thought you've reflected on, and each little doodle you've added (yes, even the questionable ones) are steps on your journey to a more positive, intentional life.

Life isn't always smooth sailing - sometimes it's more like paddling a kayak through a thunderstorm. But here's the thing: you've got the tools to navigate it. Whenever the waters get choppy, remember the seven switches. Switch on appreciation to find the silver linings. Switch on mindfulness to anchor yourself in the moment. And when all else fails, grab a pen and come back to these pages - they'll always be here for you.

Positivity doesn't mean pretending everything is perfect; it means choosing to focus on the good, even when things feel tough. It's about giving yourself grace on the hard days and celebrating the small wins on the good ones. The light you've cultivated through this journal isn't something fleeting - it's part of you now. Keep nurturing it, and it will keep growing.

And remember, your light isn't just for you. The positivity you've created has a ripple effect, brightening the lives of those around you. Whether it's a kind word, a listening ear, or just showing up with a smile, you have the power to make someone's day a little better. That's pretty amazing, isn't it?

So here's to you - your courage, your curiosity, and your commitment to living with intention. Keep switching on that light of yours and trust that every step forward, no matter how small, is leading you towards a brighter, more joyful life.

With all the encouragement in the world,
Nuria

Discover the Power of Positivity with The Positivity Switch

Unlock the transformative power of positivity with The Positivity Switch, your guide to mastering mindset shifts that bring clarity, joy, and resilience to your everyday life.

In this inspiring and practical book, you'll discover:
- The Seven Switches: Learn how simple mindset shifts, from appreciation to resilience, can completely change the way you experience life.
- Actionable Tools: Packed with exercises, reflections, and real-life examples, this book will help you integrate positivity into your daily routine.
- A Science-Backed Approach: Understand the psychology behind positivity and how these practices can rewire your brain for lasting change.
- Practical Strategies for Real Life: Whether you're navigating challenges or striving for personal growth, The Positivity Switch offers the tools to guide you.

Inside the pages of this book, you'll explore how to:
- Appreciate the small joys in life and cultivate gratitude.
- Reframe setbacks into opportunities with a shift in perspective.
- Build resilience to bounce back stronger after life's challenges.
- Visualise your goals and align your actions to achieve them.

This book isn't about pretending everything is perfect—it's about embracing the ups and downs of life with a mindset that helps you grow, connect, and thrive.

If this journal has inspired you, then The Positivity Switch will give you the tools to deepen your practice, understand the core principles of positivity, and create meaningful, lasting change in your life.

Grab your copy of The Positivity Switch today and take the next step in your journey toward a brighter, more positive life.